Preface

The anonymous author of the earl
Ruin', found much to say when they discovered the ruins of a
Roman city, thought to be Bath, three hundred years after it
was abandoned. The poem imagines the people who built the
town, the smiths and the masons, as well as those who lived,
ate and drank within the mead halls of this vanished society.
It was, as the poem says, 'the work of Giants', yet given its
state of ruin, just as vulnerable as humans.

I had something similar in mind when I began my
position as writer-in-residence at Seaton Delaval Hall. Although
not entirely a ruin, the Central Hall, which partly burned down
in 1822, has the air of an arcadia, reminiscent of Thomas Cole's
cycle of paintings *The Course of Empire*. There's something
deeply unsettling about seeing ruins, yet they also have a way
of firing up the imagination, speaking volumes about the human
experience, evoking the elegiac and the political and everything
in between.

Like 'The Ruin', I wanted to think about life as it was
lived here. Originally, I set out to write from the perspectives
of the muses who stand as silent witnesses inside the Central
Hall. But after meeting many inspiring people – ecologists,
archaeologists, gardeners and volunteers – who were kind
enough to share their knowledge, I found another way to go.

Suddenly, Seaton Delaval Hall came alive with the
voices of those who work here now, as well as those throughout
the ages. I could see it: the entire Hall drawn out of the landscape
that surrounds it like a sudden act of creation. I could hear the
many generations of men and women whose lives depended
upon its existence speaking at once. With their voices in my

head, I immediately set about writing; usually in the car after an inspiring conversation about the history of the landscape, the family and their industrial interests.

It is impossible to provide a definitive account of such a long period of time and a family who has occupied this patch of the North East of England since the Norman conquest. But I hope that this small collection of poems provides an introduction to another perspective from which to think about the multi-faceted history and ongoing life of Seaton Delaval Hall.

Walk around the grounds, speak to those who work here and listen to what the statues or the stonework or the Ha-Has have to say. Even when it's silent, there are voices everywhere.

John Challis, February 2022

Contents

Winter Opening Hours

You don't notice when they're there
but when they're gone, and all around
you see the things you didn't:
clouds and markings on the stone,
acanthus on the columns, mushrooms
on the lawn. I've only felt this way
once or twice, so quiet and so alone.
The voices in my head downed
their thoughts and stood as I stood
at the gates, the key light in my hand,
the John Deere purring behind.
I wanted *then* to last longer than it could
which is what it felt like standing there,
the key heavy in my mind, calling
me back to the life that I was living
before I came to lock the gates
and realised I was breathing, not the air
but silence, before the night falls.

Hallsong

landowner, groundskeeper,
quarryman and miner,
bottle-smith, salt designer,
clinker-monger, harbour;

party house, theatre maker,
writer's bank and legislator,
Pan impresario,
comedian and trickster;

fire-breather, burn-survivor,
nursery and batcave,
a hidey hole for nature,
proprietor of mud;

rosarium and gardener,
archivist and Playdium,
a tough guy by the water,
a tender, ruined god.

What we know

The Ecologist

No one knows, but access to the gardens
must be through the gaps in window frames
we're yet to find. And what we know
is never right: we do not know if each one
has a pattern like a fingerprint upon
the wing, and if these markings are unique.
They live inside the joist holes and in
the cracks where concrete's dried and fled,
and eat three thousand midges daily.
We shine our lights and want to know
the noises, are they general or specific?
Do they wake as children do in darkness
and call out for their parents? It must be like a city,
all of them barrelling through the rush hours
of dawn and dusk towards their long nap
in the walls, when they'll drop their temperature
and show as blue lumps on the sensor
so we cannot tell the life and stone apart.

Ha-Ha

You do not see us coming but we see you
marching purposefully across the lawn
to where the hares frolic and the huntress
is sentry or once was when Pan believed

the woods and all the does were his
and not some Delavals or others, when land
was land and no man's, and we a natural plunge,
before the spade, before the kiln,

when we were ditch and not some trap
to hold the sheep and horses back
and not some trick of green on green to make it
look like everything is yours and yours alone.

The best is still below

The Archaeologist

We dig or else conduct a survey
and bit by bit fetch up things
born or created. Our work is time,
time it takes to know the layers

time has laid. We hope our shovels
aren't like fires and alkaline
exists to keep the skulls and femurs,
so we can carbon date the teeth

or else the pollen, dispersed
between strata. We are not miners
but disciples, and work to spread
belief in land not as commercial

but as sacred interest. Though
pollen isn't femur nor is pollen
artefact, so much is in the earth
and rarely cash to resurrect it

and it's safer there, where land
still belongs to land. Our only hope
is to show an extract, played back
on the widescreen of the ground.

The Servants

With no means of getting out
or anywhere, to walk for miles

is to court a cold that takes
a while, comes in waves, shivers

off the spirit like a cat does
water when it rains, no port

nor cottage in the forest,
which is how it feels to have

fields beyond boundaries
and clouds that turn the land

around, and further fields
where no one knows our name

or cares or thinks or speaks as we
nobodies from the big house.

Letter from a Farmer

My Lord,
            only in our poems do we possess
the romance of the plough. The page becomes
the field on which we sow our only value.
No wonder why the men without
beg for your patronage. There's much of you
but none of us. We leave the ditch
along the boundary and the avenue of oak.
Though think me not ungrateful.
There is a beauty order makes and I thank you
for your kingdom's trust. I only ask
to be acknowledged. Like stone masons
and labourers, I made your world possible,
and England a heaven where I too exist.

Underhouse

I must have been a stone once,
satisfied with stillness. I watch the dark
dilute the corridors and can hold

this pose for hours. There's pleasure
in being anchored. Not many stay
down for long. Like 'moles' one said,

another, 'worms', they march
up the stairs as lords into the light.
I like it here. I know my place.

Conductor

Edward Delaval

I go up high to feel the wind
when wind does what wind does,
fast and low and furious, rain
is grit, is glass, and try to keep

my head up, try not to move
an inch, and I do this while
I hold my hands up like a fin
and beg, pray, and beg for it,

lightning head to toe along
the conduit I call myself.
Since summer started, I've
been among the Putti, spine

alert to rumbles, to see inside
the second lightning strikes,
to see the ground below alive
like fire in the August pines,

the mud tracks and hedgerows
bright as molten glass,
to see the country from above
electrify the land.

Closing Night

3rd January 1822

Even if I go unnoticed, I know
I played my part, the riot of my younger days
seared their years into the stone

and now here at the curtain call
I watch my work and rise condemned
to drown inside my own updraft.

Here's the world I might have known,
woods and fields and open time
had nature cast me differently, as, say,

a blade of grass and not the spark
applauding in the chimney of the *one-
night-only* theatre of the north.

A Way of Knowing

Sometimes, when it's only me inside the hall,
no cars on The Avenue, slow days when the rain's hard,
the farmer's out on Lumpwell Field ploughing
earth or seeding ground, his tractor wreathed in gulls,

I think of them – the muses – their tireless night
through pit disasters, grieving mothers, parties,
fire, blackout, war. I think of them, these mysteries
niched in Vanbrugh's vision, but nonetheless here,

and I watch them while the rain falls, while the bats
begin to fidget inside their homes inside the walls,
and know these plaster effigies are just as good

as any faith one might employ to find one's place
in the empty hall of history. Stone is turning into wing
behind the cracking robes. I sit here and I listen.

The Mausoleum

Today I wore good boots to cross
the fields of fallen trees, taproots
against the wind, to find the hidden
Mausoleum, a hidey hole for teens.

I crossed the Ha-Has, wire fences,
stepped between the branches
on a tenant farmer's land
and found no epitaphs or caskets

but local news: who fancied who
carved into stone. Wayward
sons and daughters must have
thought themselves immortal,

high inside this tomb a father
built to mourn his Jack and high
on love with only stars, their quiet
knowledge and the creaking trees.

Built to hold, it never held, built
to mourn, it never did. Today,
after the storm, I came and found
this poem sleeping in the crypt.

Notes

What we know
This poem adapts information spoken to me by Tina Wiffen, an ecologist working at Seaton Delaval Hall to monitor and protect the population of pipistrelle bats living in the walls.

Ha-Ha
A statue of Pan once stood within the walled garden (now the car park) at Seaton Delaval Hall.

The best is still below
This poem is inspired by speaking to Mark Newman, an archaeologist who has worked for the National Trust since 1988.

Letter from a Farmer
Although no such letter exists, I was compelled to write one after spending time reading letters in the Delaval archive, which is held within Northumberland Archives at Woodhorn Museum.

Conductor
Edward Delaval was a member of a committee appointed to recommend ways to protect St Paul's Cathedral from a lightning strike. He made sure that Seaton Delaval Hall was one of the first buildings in the country to have a lighting conductor fitted.

Closing Night
The Central Hall was almost burned to the ground on 3rd January 1822. It is said that servants and local people rallied to save items, such as papers, from the building.

The Mausoleum
Built as a memorial to John 'Jack' Delaval, the only son of Sir John Hussey Delaval, the Mausoleum was never consecrated and so never used.

Acknowledgements

There are many people to whom I owe my gratitude. Without conversations with volunteers and historians, ecologists and gardeners, archaeologists and curators, I would not have been able to write these poems. They are my co-creators and deserve recognition as well as my apologies for borrowing snatches of their speech or misrepresenting the facts in the name of poetry. In particular, I wish to thank:

Chris Brock for his support and enthusiasm, and for showing me the Mausoleum and carrying the ladder; Elspeth Gould for her research and time in explaining the history of the Hall in all its magnificent detail; Mark Newman for informing and shaping my understanding of archaeology; Tina Wiffen for introducing me to the pipistrelles in the walls; and Dr Helen Williams for sharing her research into literary figures at the Hall. The worlds that all of you have introduced me to have shaped my understanding of Seaton Delaval Hall in ways I could not have imagined.

Many thanks to Leigh Boyd, Imogen Cloët, Susan Dungworth, Siobhan Falkous, Christo Wallers, Andrew Weatherhead, and the staff and volunteers at Seaton Delaval Hall. Thanks also to the writers who participated in the creative writing course: our conversations about writing and history will go on to inform and inspire my thinking. I also want to thank the members of the Northern Poetry Workshop for reading and commenting on drafts of these poems. Thanks are also due to Kris Johnson, my first reader.

Lastly, I want to acknowledge Emma Thomas and the National Trust and Anna Disley and New Writing North: their management of this residency and support for my work has made this a truly transformative experience.

Biographical note

John Challis was writer-in-residence at Seaton Delaval Hall in 2021/22 as part of the Curtain Rises project, funded by the National Lottery Heritage Fund. He is a poet, researcher and teacher living in the North East. His debut collection of poems *The Resurrectionists* was published by Bloodaxe Books in 2021. A pamphlet, *The Black Cab* (Poetry Salzburg), appeared in 2017 and was a New Writing North Read Regional title. He has received a Pushcart Prize, a Northern Writers' Award, an Authors' Foundation grant from The Society of Authors, and was highly commended in the 2021 Forward Prizes for Poetry. His work has appeared on BBC Radio 4, in *Ambit*, *The Guardian*, *Poetry Ireland Review*, *Poetry London* and elsewhere.